W9-BCR-468

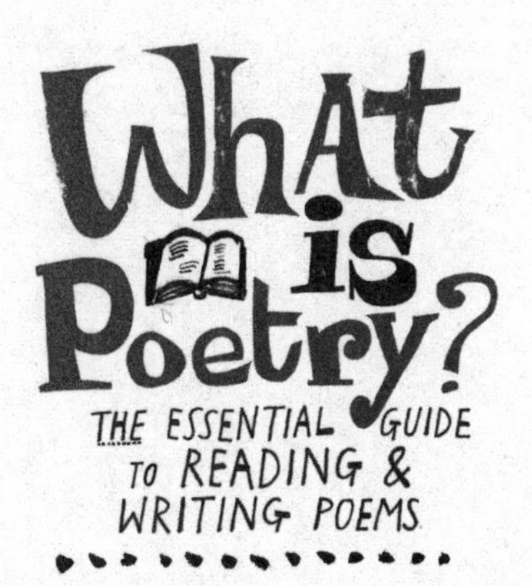
What is Poetry?
THE ESSENTIAL GUIDE
TO READING &
WRITING POEMS

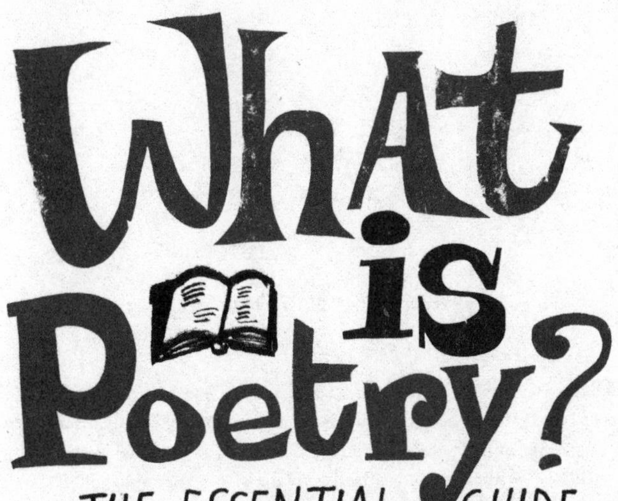

THE ESSENTIAL GUIDE TO READING & WRITING POEMS

MICHAEL ROSEN

illustrated by **Jill Calder**

CANDLEWICK PRESS

First U.S. edition 2019

Library of Congress Catalog Card Number 2018960317
ISBN 978-1-5362-0159-8 (hardcover)
ISBN 978-1-5362-0158-1 (paperback)

18 19 20 21 22 23 BVG 10 9 8 7 6 5 4 3 2 1

Printed in Berryville, VA, U.S.A.

This book was typeset in Briosio Pro.
The illustrations were done in ink.

Candlewick Press
99 Dover Street
Somerville, Massachusetts 02144

visit us at www.candlewick.com

For Emma, Elsie, and Emile

Contents

Introduction

Poetry belongs to all of us; everyone can read poems, make up poems, or share poems with others. Though we often talk about poetry being dense or difficult, poems are able to present complicated or challenging ideas in ways that we can carry around in our heads. They help us ask questions about the world, how we use words, and who we are.

This book talks about how to read, write, and listen to poetry. In the first chapter, I'll start by simply asking, What is poetry? I don't think I'll be answering that, though!

In chapter 2, I consider a more practical question: What can you do with a poem?

In chapter 3, I talk about the writing process behind some of my poems and my personal experience as a poet.

This leads me into chapter 4, where I offer a few ideas for starting poems of your own, and chapter 5, where I've collected together tips on how to write and edit your poems.

Chapter 6 gives some useful technical pointers for looking at poems.

And the last chapter I'd like to keep a surprise....

Finally, in the appendix, you'll find lots of different ways to go out and get involved in poetry — it might even be the best place to start! In fact, you can read this book in all kinds of ways: straight through, in bits, to and fro, rereading parts . . . or however you like.

I can't speak for all poets, but the main reason I write poems is that I hope they offer readers something to think about and talk about. They are a way of opening a conversation. I'd like this book to do the same — because, more than anything else, it's about enjoying poetry, and living with it and in it.

M. R.

Chapter 1

What Is Poetry?

A poem is a poem if the writer and the reader agree it's a poem. But people don't always agree, and when they argue about it, they try to find some special things about poetry that you can't find in other kinds of writing. They say things like:

- a poem has to **rhyme,** or should have a particular **rhythm;**
- a poem should have **metaphors** and **similes** (I'll be talking about these later on);
- a poem should say something beautiful in an especially beautiful way;
- a poem should say something that surprises us;
- a poem should say something in a memorable way.

One problem with this is that it's quite easy to find other kinds of writing that do some or all of these things: proverbs, riddles, jokes, plays, songs, holy writings, and speeches. And another problem is that plenty of people have written what *they* say are poems but that have no rhymes or particular rhythms, metaphors or similes, or special, beautiful language.

So answering the question What is poetry? is not easy. One way around it is to ask another question: What can poetry DO?

So I've chosen some pieces of writing that writers and readers agree are poems, and I'm going to think about what they DO and what I'm doing in my mind as I read them.

WHAT CAN POETRY DO?

Poetry Can Suggest Things

A Word Is Dead

A word is dead

When it is said,

Some say.

I say it just

Begins to live

That day.

Emily Dickinson (1830–1886)

We often think of poems as things you find in books, but most of Emily Dickinson's poems weren't published when she was alive. She wrote them at home and put them in little packets, which her sister discovered after she died.

My first reaction when I read this poem is to ask questions: Can words die? What would a dead word be? What does it mean if a word "begins to live" when it is said? What does it mean for a word to begin to live? And who is the "I" who says "I say"?

A six-line poem has gotten me asking a lot of questions. But there are no answers! When I read a story in the paper or watch the news on TV, quite often there are questions *and* answers. Let's imagine that this poem is a news item. We would be told just who it is going around claiming that words die when people say them. We would be told who the "I" is in "I say." And there's every chance that the person speaking would explain to us why saying a word will make it begin to live.

Not here, though. Not in this poem. We're just

left hanging in midair, trying to figure all this out for ourselves. So, the poem has presented some problems, we've asked some questions, and it hasn't answered any of them!

I could be very annoyed by this. On the other hand, I might realize that it's just the way some poems are. And instead of being annoyed, I could wait and see. Maybe something will crop up a few days later when I'm out and about, and I will think to myself, *That word seemed to come alive when it was said.*

And then the poem will work itself out as the days go by.

I'm going to use one word to cover everything I've said here: **suggestive.** I think a lot of poems are suggestive. They make suggestions — nothing more, nothing less. They suggest feelings, thoughts, problems, and ideas. And they don't try to give answers. They leave us to do a lot of figuring out.

WHAT CAN POETRY DO?

Poetry Can Give an Impression

From a Railway Carriage

Faster than fairies, faster than witches,

Bridges and houses, hedges and ditches;

And charging along like troops in a battle,

All through the meadows the horses and cattle:

All of the sights of the hill and the plain

Fly as thick as driving rain;

And ever again, in the wink of an eye,

Painted stations whistle by.

Here is a child who clambers and scrambles,

All by himself and gathering brambles;

Here is a tramp who stands and gazes;

And there is the green for stringing the daisies!

Here is a cart run away in the road

Lumping along with man and load;

And here is a mill and there is a river:

Each a glimpse and gone for ever!

Robert Louis Stevenson (1850–1894)

Robert Louis Stevenson wrote novels — you probably know or have heard of *Treasure Island* — but he also wrote a book of poems about his childhood, and this is one of them.

When you read it, you can try tapping the rhythm just as you might when you hear a song. You can tap four times in each line of the poem. In the first line, for example, you can tap on "Fast" in "Faster," "fair" in "fairies," "fast" in the next "faster," and "witch" in "witches." If you say "TUM" for the tap and "tee" for the parts you don't tap, it goes:

FASTer than **FAIR**ies, **FAST**er than **WITCH**es

TUM tee tee, **TUM** tee, **TUM** tee tee, **TUM** tee

I think Stevenson wrote to this rhythm because **he wanted the poem to sound like the thing he was writing about** — a train going along a track. And if you're on a train, you'll notice that there are times when your carriage has been moving at a steady pace and then suddenly the rhythm changes. Perhaps the poet wanted to show this (without telling us), because after the first five lines, the rhythm of the poem changes:

Fly as thick as driving rain

If you are tapping four TUMs to the line it goes:

FLY as **THICK** as **DRIV**ing **RAIN**

TUM tee **TUM** tee **TUM** tee **TUM**

If you are a musician, you will already know that there is something strange going on here. This line doesn't fit the rhythm. You are several "tees" short! If the taps were to come at exactly the same time as in the other lines, either you'd have to leave little pauses or you'd have to make each of the tapped words last a tiny bit longer. Either way, it sounds to me like a train when it slows down.

I call all this **giving an impression.** The poem gives the impression of something without saying that it is doing it. A lot of poems work like this, but they do it in different ways — not just with rhythms. For example, they might try to show what a stream or rush of thoughts feels like by using parts of sentences, broken-up phrases, and single words instead of whole sentences.

WHAT CAN POETRY DO?

Poetry Can Play with Words

Waltzing Matilda

Once a jolly swagman[1] camped by a billabong[2]
Under the shade of a coolibah tree,
And he sang as he watched and waited till his billy[3] boiled:
"Who'll come a-waltzing Matilda with me?"

Waltzing Matilda, waltzing Matilda
You'll come a-waltzing Matilda with me
And he sang as he watched and waited till his billy boiled:
"You'll come a-waltzing Matilda with me."

Down came a jumbuck[4] to drink at that billabong.
Up jumped the swagman and grabbed him with glee.
And he sang as he shoved that jumbuck in his tucker bag:[5]
"You'll come a-waltzing Matilda with me."

Waltzing Matilda, waltzing Matilda
You'll come a-waltzing Matilda with me
And he sang as he watched and waited till his billy boiled:
"You'll come a-waltzing Matilda with me."

Up rode the squatter,[6] mounted on his thoroughbred.[7]
Down came the troopers,[8] one, two, and three.
"Whose is that jumbuck you've got in your tucker bag?
You'll come a-waltzing Matilda with me."

Waltzing Matilda, waltzing Matilda
You'll come a-waltzing Matilda with me
And he sang as he watched and waited till his billy boiled:
"You'll come a-waltzing Matilda with me."

Up jumped the swagman and sprang into the billabong.
"You'll never take me alive!" said he.
And his ghost may be heard as you pass by that billabong:
"Who'll come a-waltzing Matilda with me?"

Banjo Paterson (1864–1941)

[1] **swagman** a traveling worker who worked on different sheep stations in the Australian countryside (or "the outback")
[2] **billabong** a pool left behind when a river has changed course
[3] **billy** a little can or pot you put on a fire to cook with
[4] **jumbuck** a kind of sheep
[5] **tucker bag** a food bag
[6] **squatter** a well-off landowner, usually English in origin
[7] **thoroughbred** a very good purebred horse
[8] **troopers** mounted police

This is just about the most famous piece of writing to come from Australia. Some Australians call it their unofficial national anthem.

In the story, a traveling worker puts a sheep in his bag. He isn't really allowed to do that — the sheep seems to belong to a landowner. Rather than be captured (and imprisoned, or even sentenced to death?), the swagman drowns himself in the billabong. Then his ghost can be heard singing "Waltzing Matilda" to anyone who passes by.

Stealing animals that belong to others is called poaching. There's a long history of poaching songs, and most of them are on the side of the poachers, sympathizing with them as poor people who get food by stealing animals from rich landowners. Imagine how difficult life would be as a swagman, looking after someone else's animals while you're hungry or even starving. It makes me think of an old, old idea that animals are part of a "common treasury," a resource for everyone — and it's not fair or right for any one person to say they own them and to start fencing them in.

There's a mysterious phrase that I've never really understood at the heart of the song: "Who'll come a-waltzing Matilda with me?" It only makes sense if there is a thing you can do that isn't just "waltzing" but "waltzing Matilda." You can, as the poem says, go "waltzing Matilda" with someone, just as you might, perhaps, say that you went "dancing Harry" with someone. Can we piece together what this strange phrase means just from the poem? Or do we have to look it up online or ask someone?

The first time we hear it, the swagman is waiting for his billy to boil. The second time, he sings it to the jumbuck just as he's shoving it into his tucker bag. The third time, the troopers and the squatter say it to him — and it's a command rather than a question. The fourth time, it's the ghost singing it to anyone passing by the billabong.

Can you think of a phrase that could replace

"Who'll come a-waltzing Matilda with me?" and still more or less make sense? How about "Who'll come along with me?" It makes sense, but it doesn't give any idea of dancing. "Who'll mess around with me?" or "Who'll have fun with me?" would work quite well . . . but neither has the zip and swagger of "Who'll come a-waltzing Matilda with me?"

A whole song about a serious life-and-death conflict over work and food is given a comic touch with that one odd phrase. It's used in different ways in the poem: for example, the troopers seem to use it to mean "we caught you." A French policeman once said to me, "You will have to spend a good night in the cells if you don't carry the right papers." He meant the opposite of what he said: it wouldn't be a good night at all. It's the same with those troopers: the swagman wouldn't end up "waltzing Matilda" in the police cells either.

And I don't suppose meeting a ghost (if we believe in such things) would have you "waltzing Matilda"—

or would it? Is that the fun of the whole song? We end up waltzing Matilda along with the ghost of a poacher, celebrating his cheekiness, his nerve, his determination never to be caught alive and humiliated with a prison sentence.

What Can Poetry DO?

Poetry Can Be Symbolic

The Eagle

He clasps the crag with crooked hands;
Close to the sun in lonely lands,
Ring'd with the azure[1] world, he stands.

The wrinkled sea beneath him crawls;
He watches from his mountain walls,
And like a thunderbolt he falls.

Alfred, Lord Tennyson (1809–1892)

[1] **azure** bright blue

I like to watch TV shows about animals and birds. I've noticed that the narrators often give animals human reasons for doing things. They give names to the animals and say things like "Old Babu is missing Rama . . ." But we don't really know whether the animals are missing their friends or not. It's just something we say in order to make them seem more like humans.

At first glance, this poem isn't like that at all. But look more closely at the line "He watches from his mountain walls." You might point out that mountains aren't really walls — walls are made by humans. And whatever these walls are, they don't belong to the eagle. Eagles can't own walls.

The poet also tells us that the eagle has crooked hands. Does this mean he's old? He tells us the eagle lives close to the sun and watches over the world beneath him. He owns those mountain walls that I mentioned — which I'm guessing are cliffs — and when he falls, he's like a thunderbolt.

All this makes the eagle seem very important, as

if he is some kind of old king or lord ruling over an ancient landscape — a place that existed when the only things were the sun, the mountains, the sea, and the weather, and there were no people at all. So Tennyson has turned the eagle into a person (see **per-sonification** on page 169) and then into a **symbol** of power.

As it happens, eagles have been symbolic throughout history, and people all over the world use their image to make themselves seem powerful. Governments put eagles on coins, passports, flags, and all sorts of other things. For similar reasons, lots of schools and sports teams have eagles as their mascots.

What Can Poetry DO?

Poetry Can Be Personal

How Do I Love Thee?

How do I love thee?[1] Let me count the ways.
I love thee to the depth and breadth and height
My soul can reach, when feeling out of sight
For the ends of being and ideal grace.
I love thee to the level of every day's
Most quiet need, by sun and candle-light.
I love thee freely, as men strive for right.
I love thee purely, as they turn from praise.
I love thee with the passion put to use
In my old griefs, and with my childhood's faith.
I love thee with a love I seemed to lose
With my lost saints. I love thee with the breath,
Smiles, tears, of all my life; and, if God choose,
I shall but love thee better after death.

Elizabeth Barrett Browning (1806–1861)

[1] **thee** you

In "How Do I Love Thee?," Elizabeth Barrett Browning seems to be doing what many poets have done for the last few hundred years: **being personal.** Poets often describe the way they feel, or tell a story that has happened to them, or describe something that they've seen or heard.

Do you think Elizabeth Barrett Browning wants us to think the "I" refers to her personally? If so, she appears to be talking to one other person — and she wants to show her loving side, doesn't she? She's going to make a list of all the different ways in which she loves "thee." But it's not a real private conversation. It's as if there's a hidden part to it that says something like "Here's a personal thought that I'm going to share with whoever would like to read it."

The word "I" nearly always appears in poems like this, and it feels like we should take the "I" to mean the person writing the poem. But of course the poet is showing only a tiny part of themselves — the part expressed by the words of the poem. So we can, if we want to, guess why they have chosen to show this particular part and leave out or hide other parts.

When a poem seems to be talking to someone directly, it has the advantage of allowing a reader or listener to think about whether they are anything like the people in the poem. The "I" loves "thee" very much. They tell us how. And we might wonder if we love anyone like that. Or if we don't, might we one day in the future, or did we used to in the past? Often, poems say things that you yourself find hard to put into words — and you might feel that they've said what you wanted to say better than you could ever say it.

WHAT CAN POETRY DO?

Poetry Can Borrow Voices

Here's the opening of "My Last Duchess" by Robert Browning, who was born in 1812, lived most of his life in England and Italy, and died in 1889:

> **That's my last Duchess painted on the wall,**
> **Looking as if she were alive.**

From these first two lines, the poem sounds like a speech from a play. And as we read or listen to them, we begin to imagine who's speaking, what they're thinking, and what their motives are. The poet has taken on the voice and personality of someone and created what is called a **monologue.**

If someone is talking about their "last Duchess," we might expect that the person speaking is a duke, married to a duchess. The phrase "painted on the wall" suggests straightaway that there is a portrait of this duchess, either painted straight onto the wall—which is called a fresco—or a picture in a frame. "Looking as if she were alive" makes me think that the duchess must be dead, but does "last," which is a bit strange, mean that there were other duchesses before this one? Or that there is another one on the way? And who is this duke talking to, anyway? He sounds a bit like a guide taking us around a stately home.

So, just from the opening we can see that Robert Browning has **borrowed a voice.** He wasn't a duke and he wasn't married to a duchess — in fact, he was married to Elizabeth Barrett Browning, who wrote "How Do I Love Thee?" Through the voice he's borrowed, we can start to build up a story about what's going on: what the person speaking really thinks and who's there with them. Poets are very good at borrowing voices and, indeed, borrowing language from anywhere and everywhere — ads, prayers, rules, lullabies — and borrowing poem forms like **sonnets, limericks,** and **ballads.**

In the poem, it seems as if something rather nasty has happened. The way Robert Browning has written the speech, it's as if the duke is saying that he has done something awful to his "last" duchess, so his next duchess had better watch out. Trying to figure out what he's done, why he's done it, and who exactly he's talking to is a bit like watching a whodunit movie and trying to figure out who committed the crime and why.

It's a difficult poem, but it's worth reading the whole thing. . . .

My Last Duchess

That's my last Duchess painted on the wall,

Looking as if she were alive. I call

That piece a wonder, now; Fra Pandolf's[1] hands

Worked busily a day, and there she stands.

Will't[2] please you sit and look at her? I said

"Fra Pandolf" by design,[3] for never read

Strangers like you that pictured countenance,[4]

The depth and passion of its earnest glance,

But to myself they turned (since none puts by

The curtain I have drawn for you, but I)

And seemed as they would ask me, if they durst,[5]

How such a glance came there; so, not the first

[1] **Fra Pandolf** a painter

[2] **will't** will it

[3] **by design** on purpose

[4] **countenance** face

[5] **durst** dared

Are you to turn and ask thus. Sir, 'twas not

Her husband's presence only, called that spot

Of joy into the Duchess' cheek: perhaps

Fra Pandolf chanced to say "Her mantle[6] laps

Over my lady's wrist too much," or "Paint

Must never hope to reproduce the faint

Half-flush that dies along her throat": such stuff

Was courtesy, she thought, and cause enough

For calling up that spot of joy. She had

A heart—how shall I say?—too soon made glad,

Too easily impressed; she liked whate'er[7]

She looked on, and her looks went everywhere.

This means "made the duchess blush."

[6] **mantle** cloak

The duke thinks the duchess was too easily flattered, and he's hinting that she flirted with everyone.

[7] **whate'er** whatever

Sir, 'twas all one! My favour[8] at her breast,

The dropping of the daylight in the West,

The bough of cherries some officious[9] fool

Broke in the orchard for her, the white mule

She rode with round the terrace—all and each

Would draw from her alike the approving speech,

Or blush, at least. She thanked men—good! but thanked

Somehow—I know not how—as if she ranked[10]

My gift of a nine-hundred-years-old name

With anybody's gift. Who'd stoop to blame

This sort of trifling? Even had you skill

In speech—(which I have not)—to make your will

Quite clear to such an one, and say, "Just this

[8] **favour** a love token (probably a ribbon)

[9] **officious** self-important

He says she was so over-the-top that when she thanked men for any small gift it seemed as though that gift was just as important to her as the duke's ancient family name (which he gave her when they married).

[10] **ranked** rated

He's saying he wouldn't lower himself to her level by telling her off.

Or that in you disgusts me; here you miss,

Or there exceed the mark"—and if she let

Herself be lessoned[11] so, nor plainly set

Her wits to yours, forsooth,[12] and made excuse,[13]

—E'en[14] then would be some stooping; and I choose

Never to stoop. Oh, sir, she smiled, no doubt,

Whene'er I passed her; but who passed without

Much the same smile? This grew; I gave commands;

Then all smiles stopped together. There she stands

As if alive. Will't please you rise? We'll meet

In archery, "exceed the mark" means to shoot an arrow past a target. So he's saying the duchess sometimes misjudged things or went over the top.

[11] **lessoned** told off

This means "if she didn't argue with you."

[12] **forsooth** in truth

[13] **made excuse** said sorry

[14] **e'en** even

This means "orders." But what orders?!

The company below, then. I repeat,

The Count your master's known munificence[15]

Is ample warrant[16] that no just pretence

Of mine for dowry[17] will be disallowed;

Though his fair daughter's self, as I avowed

At starting, is my object. Nay, we'll go

Together down, sir. Notice Neptune,[18] though,

Taming a sea-horse, thought a rarity,

Which Claus of Innsbruck[19] cast in bronze for me!

[15] **munificence** wealth

[16] **ample warrant** good guarantee

[17] **dowry** money (or property) a bride brings her husband when they get married

The duke's saying, "I know the count's rich enough to pay me a lot of money if I marry his daughter. But, as I said from the beginning, I'm much more interested in the girl than the money."

[18] **Neptune** a statue of Neptune, the Roman god of the sea

[19] **Claus of Innsbruck** a sculptor

What Can Poetry DO?

Poetry Can Capture a Moment

Who Has Seen the Wind?

Who has seen the wind?

Neither I nor you:

But when the leaves hang trembling,

The wind is passing through.

Who has seen the wind?

Neither you nor I:

But when the trees bow down their heads,

The wind is passing by.

Christina Rossetti (1830–1894)

Let's imagine that we are going to have a science lesson about the wind. First, we'll think about how we know it's there — which means thinking about how we notice the wind. One of our senses is sight. Let's start with that. Can we see the wind? Has anyone seen the wind? No . . . but we've seen things that the wind does, like make leaves move and trees bend.

If this poem were a science lesson, we might go on to discuss wind power and energy. But as it's a poem, it seems to be moving on to something different: the leaves "hang trembling," and the trees "bow down their heads."

If you say trees have heads, then they've become a bit like people. When do people tremble and bow down their heads? When they're sad? When they're afraid? When they're in shock, or amazed by something incredible? Maybe the poem is telling us that the wind is religious in some way, because the trees are bowing down their heads to pray. Or it could be that it's reminding us how amazing the earth and its elements are.

Maybe you have other ideas, but whatever those ideas are, the poem *does* seem to be about feelings — it goes from talking about the wind to how we might feel about the wind. And it does this without saying, "The wind makes me feel sad" or "I find the wind amazing."

This poem is an example of what a lot of poems do: **they try to capture a small moment** or feeling, or a feeling about a moment, and then they freeze-frame it and invite us to think about just that little thing. And we may well find that by focusing on something small, we end up with a big thought about, say, why we're here, or what it's all for, or what life's about.

Our lives are made up of thousands of small moments, and we can, if we want to, make stories around any one of them. We can try to imagine we're talking to the person asking questions in this poem. Where are they? Indoors, looking out of the window at the trees blowing? On a campsite? In a forest? Are they a man or woman? Young or old? Who are they talking to? Why are they there? Are they sad? And what happens next?

Poem moments like this often suggest that there's a story around them — a bigger story that is never told. It's up to you whether you think about these stories or not.

What Can Poetry DO?

Poetry Can Be Ironic

Ozymandias

I met a traveller from an antique[1] land
Who said: Two vast and trunkless[2] legs of stone
Stand in the desert. Near them, on the sand,
Half sunk, a shattered visage[3] lies, whose frown,
And wrinkled lip, and sneer of cold command,
Tell that its sculptor well those passions read
Which yet survive (stamped on these lifeless things),
The hand that mocked them and the heart that fed;
And on the pedestal[4] these words appear:
"My name is Ozymandias, king of kings;
Look on my works, ye Mighty, and despair!"
Nothing beside[5] remains. Round the decay
Of that colossal[6] wreck, boundless[7] and bare,
The lone and level sands stretch far away.

Percy Bysshe Shelley (1792–1822)

[1] **antique** ancient

[2] **trunkless** without a body

[3] **visage** face

[4] **pedestal** the platform a statue rests on

[5] **beside** else

[6] **colossal** gigantic

[7] **boundless** to the horizon and beyond

The person speaking in this poem, the "I," meets a traveler who has been somewhere where there used to be an ancient civilization. The traveler tells the person that in the middle of the desert, there are the remains of a gigantic statue: two legs, a head and the platform under the statue, the "pedestal." On the pedestal, there's an inscription or message: "My name is Ozymandias, king of kings; Look on my works, ye Mighty, and despair!"

So there was once a king called Ozymandias (you pronounce his name "Ozzy-man-dee-ass") who had a motto. Let's stop for a moment and think about what kind of king would say "Look on my works, ye Mighty, and despair!" What kind of *person* would say such a thing?

If the king is telling someone who he calls "Mighty" to look on his "works" and "despair," then we can guess the king thinks he's mightier than the "Mighty"! Inscriptions on statues are often written *about* someone: "Jim Smith was a tailor," or some such. But this one sounds like it was written by King

Ozymandias himself before he died. This makes me think the king was someone who wanted the "Mighty" (and us) to know about him for a long time to come. But we can't see the king's "works"! They've gone: "Nothing beside remains," the traveler tells the "I." So the Mighty can't really despair, can they? No one can obey Ozymandias's orders anymore.

This is what's called **irony.** Irony involves words saying one thing but meaning another. We can't look on Ozymandias's works and despair, because they've all disappeared. Or if I were to say it in a modern way: "Not so mighty now, huh?"

You can go where you want to with this. My own thoughts take me to the idea that kings, generals, rulers, presidents, and prime ministers have power over people for only a while. We might obey their "cold commands" and fear them while they're in power, and yet, just like the rest of us, one day they'll end up with no power at all. It is ironic, as this poem shows, that what people say will happen and what actually happens in the end often turn out to be different.

WHAT CAN POETRY DO?

Poetry Can Make New Sense

Here's the **chorus** (a repeated part of a poem) from "The Jumblies," a **nonsense** poem by Edward Lear, who lived from 1812 to 1888:

> **Far and few, far and few,**
> **Are the lands where the Jumblies live;**
> **Their heads are green, and their hands are blue,**
> **And they went to sea in a Sieve.**

I've never met or seen a Jumbly. It's a made-up creature. But just from this little chorus, I know Jumblies have green heads and blue hands and that they don't live among us — they're in a rare and faraway place. What's more, I know they can do something that we can't do: float on water in a sieve — a sieve is a strainer or colander and, having holes, can't float. Even more impossible, it's not just floating in any old water — it's floating in the sea, which, as we know, is huge and often dangerous. Especially if you have a boat that doesn't float! We also know from this chorus that we're not talking about a lone or lonely Jumbly. There are at least two of them.

Why have I described all this? Because some people say that nonsense is about not making any sense. I don't agree. I think **nonsense is about making "new sense."** Poets who write nonsense nearly always create a new, alternate world. It makes sense so long as you are in that world. But in order for us to understand what the poet is talking about, we have to have enough things from our real world in the nonsense world. Here we've got heads, hands, colors, a sea, a sieve, and so on. These are all words and things from our world. They make sense. But in the world of this poem, the real things are jumbled up (is this a clue as to why they're called Jumblies?). So, green and blue are colors we see in the real world, but we don't usually see green heads and blue hands. We've seen sieves and boats and the sea, but we've never seen a sieve being used as a boat on the sea.

Poems are places where we can create or read about these alternate, jumbled-up worlds. When you read the whole poem, you'll find out that the Jumblies sail away for twenty years or more, even though their friends tell them not to. At times it feels like a terrifying journey. They arrive in a place where they buy an owl, silvery bees, forty bottles of "Ring-Bo-Ree," and no end of Stilton cheese. When they come back, the story of their journey seems to inspire everyone else to do the same.

This means that in among the nonsense of made-up creatures and unknown objects, there are strong (and real) feelings of risk, danger, satisfaction, and friendship in the poem. Again — not so much nonsense as new sense!

The Jumblies

I

They went to sea in a Sieve, they did,
In a Sieve they went to sea:
In spite of all their friends could say,
On a winter's morn, on a stormy day,
In a Sieve they went to sea!
And when the Sieve turned round and round,
And every one cried, "You'll all be drowned!"
They called aloud, "Our Sieve ain't big,
But we don't care a button! we don't care a fig!
In a Sieve we'll go to sea!"

Far and few, far and few,
Are the lands where the Jumblies live;
Their heads are green, and their hands are blue,
And they went to sea in a Sieve.

II

They sailed away in a Sieve, they did,
  In a Sieve they sailed so fast,
With only a beautiful pea-green veil
Tied with a riband by way of a sail,
  To a small tobacco-pipe mast;
And every one said, who saw them go,
"O won't they be soon upset, you know!
For the sky is dark, and the voyage is long,
And happen what may, it's extremely wrong
  In a Sieve to sail so fast!"

Far and few, far and few,
  Are the lands where the Jumblies live;
Their heads are green, and their hands are blue,
  And they went to sea in a Sieve.

III

The water it soon came in, it did,
The water it soon came in;
So to keep them dry, they wrapped their feet
In a pinky paper all folded neat,
And they fastened it down with a pin.
And they passed the night in a crockery-jar,
And each of them said, "How wise we are!
Though the sky be dark, and the voyage be long,
Yet we never can think we were rash or wrong,
While round in our Sieve we spin!"

Far and few, far and few,
Are the lands where the Jumblies live;
Their heads are green, and their hands are blue,
And they went to sea in a Sieve.

IV

And all night long they sailed away;
    And when the sun went down,
They whistled and warbled a moony song
To the echoing sound of a coppery gong,
    In the shade of the mountains brown.
"O Timballo! How happy we are,
When we live in a sieve and a crockery-jar,
And all night long in the moonlight pale,
We sail away with a pea-green sail,
    In the shade of the mountains brown!"

Far and few, far and few,
    Are the lands where the Jumblies live;
Their heads are green, and their hands are blue,
    And they went to sea in a Sieve.

V

They sailed to the Western Sea, they did,
    To a land all covered with trees,
And they bought an Owl, and a useful Cart,
And a pound of Rice, and a Cranberry Tart,
    And a hive of silvery Bees.
And they bought a Pig, and some green Jack-daws,
And a lovely Monkey with lollipop paws,
And forty bottles of Ring-Bo-Ree,
    And no end of Stilton Cheese.

Far and few, far and few,
Are the lands where the Jumblies live;
Their heads are green, and their hands are blue,
And they went to sea in a Sieve.

VI

And in twenty years they all came back,

In twenty years or more,

And every one said, "How tall they've grown!"

For they've been to the Lakes, and the Torrible Zone,

And the hills of the Chankly Bore;

And they drank their health, and gave them a feast

Of dumplings made of beautiful yeast;

And every one said, "If we only live,

We too will go to sea in a Sieve,—

To the hills of the Chankly Bore!"

Far and few, far and few,

Are the lands where the Jumblies live;

Their heads are green, and their hands are blue,

And they went to sea in a Sieve.

What Can Poetry DO?

Poetry Can Make Familiar Things Feel Unfamiliar & Unfamiliar Things Feel Familiar

Now I'm going to look at two speeches by William Shakespeare (1564–1616). They are spoken by characters in the middle of plays, so perhaps they're not poems but what we might call **poetic writing.** I've included them because I'm very fond of them, and they remind me of what language can do.

Be not afeard.[1] The isle is full of noises,
Sounds, and sweet airs,[2] that give delight and hurt not.
Sometimes a thousand twangling instruments
Will hum about mine ears, and sometime voices
That if I then had waked after long sleep
Will make me sleep again; and then, in dreaming
The clouds methought[3] would open and show riches
Ready to drop upon me, that when I waked
I cried to dream again.

The Tempest, Act 3, Scene 2

[1] **afeard** afraid

[2] **airs** melodies

[3] **methought** I thought

These words are spoken by a character named Caliban in a play called *The Tempest.* He was born on a magical island, which means he is a native or an indigenous person of the island. He thinks that the island belongs to him, but years ago a duke and his daughter were shipwrecked there and enslaved Caliban. He deeply regrets having taught the duke how to survive on the island by showing him where to find fresh water and which plants to eat.

Early on in the play, the duke's old enemies arrive, and Caliban becomes friends with two men who work for them, hoping that the three of them can lead a revolt against the duke. In this strange place, the two men are fearful. Imagine you were suddenly to arrive on a tropical island and hear all sorts of strange noises. You're in an unfamiliar place and you feel very afraid, but someone who has lived there since he was born reassures you. He does it not just by saying, "Don't worry," but by telling the two men how he felt when he first heard noises on the island. It's almost as if he is bringing them news from a strange place and trying to get them to understand him — and to understand that they are not in danger. You could call this **making the unfamiliar familiar.**

Poets often do this in poems. They write about odd, strange, bizarre, extraordinary, or terrible things in such a way that we can see, hear, feel, and understand them. Some of the most famous examples of this are poems written by soldiers during and after the First World War — poems that showed people who had no idea what modern, industrial trench warfare was like, just how horrible and awful it was.

The second speech, from Shakespeare's play *Macbeth,* does the opposite: **it makes familiar things seem unfamiliar.** Macbeth is a Scottish nobleman who is told by three witches that one day he will be king. To make sure this happens, he kills the king, assumes the throne himself, and sends murderers after those who might challenge his rule.

Now, I've never been told that I'm going to be king. I've never *wanted* to be king. I've never murdered anyone. I don't know what any of these things would feel like. But Shakespeare invites us to imagine what it might be like in a speech where Macbeth tells the audience what he's thinking after the murders.

Tomorrow, and tomorrow, and tomorrow,
Creeps in this petty pace from day to day
To the last syllable of recorded time,
And all our yesterdays have lighted fools
The way to dusty death. Out, out, brief candle.
Life's but a walking shadow, a poor player[1]
That struts and frets his hour upon the stage,
And then is heard no more. It is a tale
Told by an idiot, full of sound and fury,
Signifying[2] nothing.

Macbeth, Act 5, Scene 5

[1] **player** actor
[2] **signifying** that means

Before I heard this speech, I never thought that something as familiar as "tomorrow" could creep. I didn't think of the past as "all our yesterdays." I didn't think that those yesterdays could "light" me (or "fools") toward death (is Shakespeare saying our yesterdays are like candles?).

So, by saying that one thing is like another, something as familiar as time can start to feel strange. But there are other strangenesses, too. Shakespeare repeats words in a way that makes language itself seem new and unfamiliar.

We all know people who say things like "Never, never, never, in all my life!" or "I don't believe it, I really don't believe it. . . ." But I've never heard anyone say, "Tomorrow, and tomorrow, and tomorrow." Poets often use familiar words in new and strange ways that make us think differently about the words and what they mean. Yes, we all know that tomorrow is going to happen tomorrow! And we know that the day after, it's going to be another tomorrow. But if I say, "Tomorrow and tomorrow and tomorrow," I give a sense that the days are dragging ahead of me before I've even gotten to them. And there's something unstoppable about the repetition — it's a bit like a drum or hammer, banging it into me that time's going on and on and on.

Isn't it amazing that Shakespeare has done this simply by repeating a word that we all know, a word we use all the time without really thinking about it? In fact, we nearly always use the word *tomorrow* in order to talk about something else. We say, "I'll see you tomorrow," or "I'll go shopping tomorrow." By repeating it, Shakespeare asks us to think about the tomorrow-ness of tomorrows!

Macbeth goes on to say the tomorrows are creeping from "day to day," and in a flash he's talking about "yesterdays." Pause for a moment: these different words — tomorrow, day, and yesterday — are all about the same thing . . . a day. But by putting them so closely together, Shakespeare's got me thinking about days and time in a new way.

Then Macbeth talks of "the last syllable of recorded time." When I hear "last syllable," I think about the very last sound of a piece of writing, the last part of the last word of the last chapter of a book, and the last bit of meaning or thought I get from that very last moment. But Macbeth says it's the last syllable of time. Hang on — time doesn't have syllables. It has years, months, days, hours, minutes, and seconds. By saying "the last syllable of recorded time," he puts a word about writing ("syllable") with time in what we might say is an impossible way. It doesn't make sense. And yet, we can imagine the idea of time (or our time on earth) coming to an end with a syllable rather than a second. Or, we can merge and blur words ("syllables") with time. Time can seem as if it's the passing of our thoughts. Or our thoughts can seem like the passing of time.

By giving Macbeth a speech in which he talks about the passing of time in a strange and unfamiliar way, Shakespeare brings us closer to a totally unfamiliar kind of person: a murderer who wants to be king.

Chapter 2

What Can You Do with a Poem?

Sometimes the best way to understand poems is through doing things with them. This chapter talks about some of the things you can do. You might be able to think of others.

Read It!

This may sound obvious, but one of the first things to do with a poem is to just read it, without doing anything to it or with it. Just read it. Then read it again. And even read it a third time. Every time I've read a poem — even one of my own — more than once, doors start to open for me. It's as if I walk into another room and find a bit more of it each time. That's because poems often say things in strange ways. Reading them several times means that they become less strange.

You can read poems quietly to yourself. Or you can read them out loud. You can mumble them under your breath, just letting the feeling of them run out of your mouth. Or, if you want to, you can perform them. This may mean putting on different kinds of voices: loud or soft, sad or happy, calm or angry, serious or jokey. . . . If you're reading a poem with

someone else or in a group, you can break it into different parts, with one person reading one part and another person reading another. You can think of it as a little play. You don't have to stick to the exact words. You can pull out several parts and whisper them. You can echo words that someone else has just said, or say some of the words solo and others together.

Ask Questions

As you read a poem, you can ask yourself: What does this remind me of? Is there anything in it that reminds me of something that has happened to me or to someone I know? How does it remind me? If you're with other people, you can talk about the different things the poem makes you think of. You can just talk about them or write them down. If you're interested in writing poems yourself, then keeping a note of these things will help.

Some people might think this is pointless or has nothing to do with what the poem is about. I say it has everything to do with it. Poems are ways of opening conversations with readers. The poem "talks" to something in us. That something in us reacts to what's in the poem, just as we might react when someone throws us a ball. And the something is made up of all the things we've done in our lives — our experience. The poem "talks" to our experience, so by asking ourselves what it reminds us of, we are bringing to the surface how the poem reaches us.

You can also ask yourself: Does the poem remind me of another poem, a story, movie, TV show, song, painting, or dance? Again, if this seems to have nothing to do with what the poem is about, I'd say it has everything to do with it. No poem sits in the world separate from the other artistic things we do. When we read a poem, our reaction to it is partly based on these things: the songs, movies, paintings, and TV shows that we've seen or heard. If you're with someone else, or in a group, it's great to share all this, and talk about how or why the poem reminded you of something in particular.

Poems make us want to ask all sorts of other questions, too: What does that mean? Why did she say that? What's the point of that? And hundreds of others. You can collect these. You can write them down. Maybe you have questions for the person who wrote the poem. Write them down. If you're with someone else, or in a group, you can share them.

You don't have to be in any hurry to answer your questions. Let them hang in the air while you think about them. One or two may start to appear more important than others. If you're with someone else, maybe they can answer yours and you can answer theirs. If there are some questions that you really want answers to, try to find ways of getting them answered — the Internet is one very likely place, and someone who has read a lot of poetry might also help. Some questions about poems have no answers, or several answers. That's fine. And a good number of poems don't have definite yes or no, right or wrong, answers. That's fine, too!

Look for Connections

Poems bring words together using what I call **secret strings.** You might find a secret string when:

- one word sounds like another — this could be because they rhyme or because they begin with the same letter (**alliteration**) or use the same vowel sound (**assonance**).
- the rhythm of one line is the same as the rhythm of another line.

- words (or groups of words) are repeated.
- some kind of word picture is built up by using the same words or similar words. So, for example, the poem might repeat the idea of things being bright or light or shining or dazzling. The repetition creates a picture. Pictures like this are called the poem's **imagery.**
- there are opposites. If, say, one part of a poem is about birth and another part has something to do with death, then there's a secret string running between those different parts of the poem.

Remember, these strings belong to you. They may be strings that the poet had in mind — but maybe not. Sometimes poets don't realize that they're stringing different parts of a poem together. When you spot secret strings, you are like a poem detective, hunting down clues as to how the poem is held together.

On the next two pages, I'm doing just that with a poem by Thomas Hardy. . . .

Snow in the Suburbs

Every branch big with it,

Bent every twig with it;

Every fork like a white web-foot;

Every street and pavement mute:

Some flakes have lost their way, and grope back upward, when

Meeting those meandering down they turn and descend again.

The palings are glued together like a wall,

And there is no waft of wind with the fleecy fall.

A sparrow enters the tree,
Whereon immediately

A snow-lump thrice his own slight size
Descends on him and showers his head and eyes,

And overturns him,
And near inurns him,
And lights on a nether twig, when its brush
Starts off a volley of other lodging lumps with a rush.

The steps are a blanched slope,
Up which, with feeble hope,
A black cat comes, wide-eyed and thin;
And we take him in.

Thomas Hardy (1840–1928)

Strings 1 and 2: RHYTHM and SOUND

In this poem, rhythm and sound work together in very clever ways. Every two lines rhyme, so we might expect the poem to have a neat, regular rhythm. But even though the opening lines have a steady beat, supported by the repeated consonant sounds "Every branch big with it, | Bent every twig with it," the rhythm changes in the third line — and then continues to shift as the poem goes on.

In the two longest lines "Some flakes have lost their way, and grope back upward, when | Meeting those meandering down they turn and descend again," the rhythm itself begins to "meander," switching from one pattern to the next. It's almost as if the poem is acting out the whirling of the snowflakes, changing direction over and over. But the "when"/"again" rhyme keeps these lines tied together.

We then meet two animals: a sparrow and a black cat. They are introduced separately, each time at the beginning of a line. This shows us that both creatures are all alone, two tiny dots in a vast white landscape.

So they seem to mirror each other, as if they are part of a pattern. The sounds of the poem emphasize this, for example when the repetition of "him" in the description of the sparrow is like the rhyme for the cat: "thin"/"in."

But the use of "we" in the last line changes things. This is the first time we're told someone is watching all this, and it's a "we" rather than a single "I." This makes the creatures seem even lonelier, by comparison. Sometimes a poet sets up a pattern then breaks it to surprise the reader or to create contrast.

String 3: IMAGERY

Poets often make their rhythm and sound strings go along with the images or pictures they give us. When you read the poem, it helps to try to picture the scene as it unfolds. We begin with a wide shot of a white landscape. There's snow as far as the eye can see, on "every branch," "every twig," "every fork," "every street and pavement" . . . everywhere! But then in the second verse, the poem zooms in on a single sparrow (one tiny speck of gray, black, and brown in the middle of all that white). He lands on a snowy branch and sets off a mini avalanche. This moment feels very dramatic: the repetition of "and" raises the pace, and "inurns" means "to bury," so for a second it seems like the sparrow is in real trouble.

But without finding out what happens to the sparrow, we move away in the next verse to focus on a black cat climbing a set of "blanched" (whitened) stairs. We're told it's "wide-eyed and thin" and it seems vulnerable, climbing the steps with "feeble hope." Then, in the final line, the speaker says, "And we take him in." It's the shortest line of the poem and all the words are one syllable long, which means it has its own unique rhythm. As it's also the first time "we" is used, it seems to suggest that the lonely black cat is taken out of the cold and into a warm home, to be looked after by a family (the "we").

But as the line is so vague, you can read it to mean all kinds of things—"And we take him in" could also invite us, the readers, to "take in" the cat as well!

Learn It by Heart

People say that it's important to memorize poems. I think differently. I reckon it's important only when it's important to you. So if you love a poem, you might want to learn it by heart. One way to find out if it's important is to practice saying it out loud, playing around with voices and parts in the ways I've suggested.

If you do want to learn a poem by heart, the best way to do it is first to read it over and over again. Second, try saying it with the poem covered up. Every time you get stuck, have a look at where you went wrong, then cover the poem again and carry on. When you've gotten to the end, start again.

It's not really a good idea to learn a poem bit by bit. If you do, you'll miss what links one part of it to the next. Reading the whole thing and trying to say it all over and over again will help it stick in your mind as a complete poem.

Doing all these things with poems — reading and rereading them, asking questions, finding secret strings, and learning them by heart (if you want!) — will help you enjoy, get to know, and make sense of them. If you do these things with another person or several people, you will often make discoveries about the poem that are exciting and amazing . . . and it's much more fun than someone lecturing you about what you are supposed to think the poem means.

Use It with Other Arts

There are all kinds of things you can do with poems involving other arts — painting, drawing, music, pottery, dance, mime, drama, film, animation, singing, tapestry, embroidery . . . and any other art that you can think of.

You can draw or paint something to do with a poem in a sketchbook or on a piece of paper — then put your picture up anywhere you like. The picture can be separate from the poem, or you can mix the words and pictures together. You could try painting the words of the poem using different lettering. One of the world's most famous poets, William Blake, did this with his poems.

If you like making things out of clay or cloth or making models, you might find a poem gives you an idea for something you can make.

Some poems go really well with music. Musical sounds can be made with instruments, your voice, or things you make out of cereal boxes, hoses, dried beans in bottles — or whatever. You can have the music in between the words, or while the words are being said, or before the poem starts, or after it finishes. Or you can pick out a word or a group of words and repeat them over and over while someone says the poem solo. If you like jazz or pop music, this will make sense to you — it's what musicians call a groove, a backing, a dub track, or a bed. It's as if you are using the repeated words as drum and bass, and the words of the poem are the melody.

Just experiment and see what sounds best. Playing with poems while performing them is a great way to get to know and understand them.

A poem, or part of a poem, might inspire you to create a dance. You might want to dance to the rhythm — or if a poem is about, say, love or anger, this might suggest a way of dancing. Or if the poem is about the sea, for example, you and a group of other people could make sea shapes while someone else recites it.

A poem might give you an idea for making up a little play, or what's called a sketch. You can recite the poem and then act out the play, or the other way around: the play and then the poem. Or you can perform a mime of the poem while it's being read aloud.

Nowadays, it's easy to make videos: just switch on your phone! You can make a movie about a poem or inspired by a poem. Or you can make a movie that runs while the poem is being said out loud — a bit like a music video.

Also, it's very easy to make slideshow presentations that you can show on your computer or a whiteboard. You can use the words of the poem with clip art (images available for free on the Internet), sounds, or whatever you like.

You can make comic strips out of a poem and turn it into a kind of graphic novel.

Imagine that you want everyone to stop and read a poem — you can make a poem poster. You'll have to think about how you want to design it, and what kinds of pictures, lettering, and colors are going to grab people's attention.

You can copy a poem and cut it up into pieces. Then you can rearrange the pieces to see if you can make them say other interesting or weird things. Or you can turn it into a game, cutting up a poem and seeing if other people can put it back into its original order.

In fact, you can do anything you want with a poem. You can ignore it, forget it, decide you don't like it — or leave it for fifty years and rediscover it later!

CHAPTER 3

MY THOUGHTS AS I WAS WRITING SOME POEMS

When we write poems, we think about what we're writing and how and why we're writing them. In this chapter, I'm sharing some thoughts with you about how I wrote a few of my poems. I hope that this will give you ideas for writing your own poems, as well as for reading other people's poetry.

I Am Angry

I am angry
Really angry
Angry, angry, angry.
I'm so angry
I'll jump up and down
I'll roll on the ground
Make a din
Make you spin
Pull out my hair
Throw you in the air
Pull down posts
Hunt down ghosts
Scare spiders
Scare tigers
Pull up trees
Bully bees
Rattle the radiators
Frighten alligators
Cut down flowers
Bring down towers
Bang all the bones
Wake up stones

Shake the tiles

Stop all smiles

Silence birds

Boil words

Mash up names

Grind up games

Crush tunes

Squash moons

Make giants run

Terrify the sun

Turn the sky red

And then go to bed.

from *A Great Big Cuddle*

A few years ago I started to write a group of poems about children talking to their toys. By the way, I don't think there's anything childish about children; I think adults and children are much more alike than people realize. What I see young children doing and saying often reminds me of what adults do and say. And the same goes for the other way around.

One day, I watched my youngest child getting angry. I know what it feels like to be angry myself, so I decided to write a poem about being angry, and I thought it would be good to start with a direct, bold statement: "I am angry." I guess in the back of my mind were two picture books I've read — one called *Angry Arthur,* and another, which had the line "Dog is hungry" in it. I also remembered a leader at a youth camp I went to when I was young who used to say, "I'm getting angry," even though he didn't sound angry at all.

I wanted the poem to explore the idea that anger takes over the whole world — just as it does in *Angry Arthur.* And if you are very little, and you know that you're small and not very powerful, being angry is in part about wishing you were bigger. I decided this needed some exaggeration. The ancient Greek name for exaggeration is **hyperbole,** which means "to throw beyond." I wanted my little person or toy to express themselves with hyperbole.

To start off, though, I decided the poem had to be more realistic so that when I began to use hyperbole it would seem surprising and funny. I also wanted the lines of the poem to sound like things a very young child would or could say: short, sharp lines. And once I got the idea of short lines, I wanted to make them rhyme. That's mostly because I wanted all the poems in the book I was writing to be a bit like chants or songs that very young children could easily learn without realizing they were learning them.

With very young children (and in actual fact with all of us sometimes), the real and the imagined can blur into each other. So it's quite likely that a very small child could "rattle radiators," but highly unlikely (though just possible) that they could or would "frighten alligators." By the time we get to "wake up stones," "stop all smiles," or "boil words," we really are in the world of the impossible — the world of hyperbole. (The line "stop all smiles" is partly borrowed from a line in a famous W. H. Auden poem, "Stop all the clocks." That's also hyperbole, which he is using to express the total grief of losing a loved one.)

By the end of the poem, the small child or toy speaking is completely in the land of hyperbole, making giants run, terrifying the sun, and turning the sky red. In the last line, I thought I would puncture all this raving and shouting with something very ordinary and safe: "And then go to bed." There's an ancient Greek name for that, too — **bathos.** It expresses the idea of coming down from a great big height to something everyday.

Maybe there's a teachery part of me that hopes that by gently laughing at one of these big rages (through hyperbole and bathos), a child will get to see his or her tantrums alongside those of the character in the poem. When people read, they compare themselves with the characters in poems and stories. And when they see the characters doing silly, dangerous, or awful things, perhaps they're warned away from doing silly, dangerous, or awful things themselves. Perhaps. Perhaps not.

Feeling Ill

Lying in the middle of the bed

waiting for the clock to change

flicking my toes on the sheets

watching a plane cross the window

staring at the glare of the light

smelling the orange on the table

counting the flowers on the curtain

holding my head with my hand

hearing the steps on the stairs

lying in the middle of the bed

waiting for the clock to change.

from *Bananas in My Ears*

I have very clear memories of what it was like being ill when I was a child. I can see myself in my bed, waiting for my mom, dad, or brother to come upstairs and bring me things or talk to me. Sometimes, as I was getting better, my parents went to work and left me on my own in the house, and the woman across the street, Mrs. Townsend, would pop over every hour or so to see if I was all right.

I started off writing this poem using a simple chorus: "I am ill." I asked myself, "What am I doing?" and wrote down a list of things. I put "I am ill" after every two or three of the answers to that question. Then I realized that the chorus broke up the rhythm.

I wanted the rhythm to be insistent and persistent — that is, to sound continuous and even tedious, just like lying in bed hour after hour. So I dropped the chorus and made a poem out of *-ing* words.

But the chorus idea stuck in my head. So after I had shuffled my answers to the "What am I doing?" question, I wanted to express the idea that it was all going on and on and on. One way to do that is to repeat at the end what you said at the beginning. It suggests that whatever you were doing at first carried on while all the other things were happening. So the lines "Lying in the middle of the bed | waiting for the clock to change" appear at the beginning and the end of the poem. That means that at the end of the poem, I'm still lying in the bed, waiting for the clock to change. And there's nothing more boring than watching a clock, waiting for it to change.

Another thing I wanted to do in this poem was express boredom without saying, "I am bored." There's absolutely nothing wrong with writing a poem that has the words "I am bored" in it. But I wanted the reader to discover that the person in the poem is bored without the person actually saying it. I like poems to challenge readers to think.

I also avoided poetic writing. I wanted the poem to sound very ordinary—sometimes I want the everyday to sound everyday and I want the emotion in the poem to come out of that everyday language and feeling.

The poem has a very regular rhythm. Each line begins with an *-ing* word, and one or two little words later there's an object that has one or two syllables. Then there are nearly always two more little words, followed by a one- or two-syllable object again. This makes the poem's rhythm nearly as regular as a clock ticking.

Fooling Around

"Do you know what?"

said Jumping John.

"I had a bellyache,

and now it's gone."

- - - - - - - -

"Do you know what?"

said Kicking Kirsty.

"All this jumping

has made me thirsty."

"Do you know what?"
said Mad Mickey.
"I sat in some glue
and I feel all sticky."

"Do you know what?"
said Fat Fred.
"You can't see me.
I'm under the bed."

from *Bananas in My Ears*

I'm very interested in nursery rhymes. They often seem to tell little dramas in very short spaces, and these very small dramas leave us with all sorts of questions that are not answered in the poem.

It's raining, it's pouring.
The old man is snoring.
He went to bed
And bumped his head,
And couldn't get up in the morning.

Once we've gotten over the idea that we don't have to take this poem seriously because it's a nursery rhyme, we might ask, What's it about? We have a sense of a setting — in the midst of a downpour — and there's an old man going to bed. For some reason, he bumps his head (on what? The headboard?), and he can't get up a few hours later. And another thing: he snores.

There's something about this downpour that conjures up another kind of downpouring — when people pour drinks down their throats. Is the old man drunk? Is that why he bumped his head and couldn't get up in the morning? Perhaps. Perhaps not.

I like trying to write little rhyming dramas like this that suggest all sorts of other things could be going on.

In the first of the Fooling Around poems, we could ask, why has John's bellyache gone? Is it because he's been jumping? Perhaps he had gas and has managed to get rid of it? In the second one, Kirsty is one of those children who carry on playing even though they should have stopped some time ago. She's only just realized she needs a drink. In the third little poem, Mickey's been messing around so much he hasn't noticed the glue — perhaps he kicked over a pot — and has ended up sitting in it. And finally, Fred tells us the very thing he's been trying to keep secret: he's under the bed.

So, there are four little stories about children playing together who find that things are going a bit wrong. I gave each of the children an alliterative name

(**J**umping **J**ohn, **K**icking **K**irsty, **M**ad **M**ickey, and **F**at **F**red) so they would sound a bit like nicknames. It makes them feel familiar. There are no adults in the poems, but I've given just a faint suggestion that at any moment an adult is going to come in and get annoyed about bedding all over the floor, jumping on beds, and glue on clothes. . . .

Short, sharp rhyming lines work rather well for this kind of little portrait. People have been writing funny little ditties in this form for hundreds of years.

Each poem begins with the same line. I did this because I thought at the time I could create a new kind of poem: a "Do you know what?" poem. I thought people would very easily pick up on it and write their own "Do you know what?" poems. Lots of teachers and children write poems that are a bit like my "Down Behind the Dustbin," poem and I thought I could give them another form to imitate.

It just goes to show that I'm affected by the way people read and use my poems. That's part of writing. It doesn't necessarily mean poets do what people tell them to or write in a way people say they like. Sometimes it does, but other times they feel like being a bit more challenging, and think, "You may have liked that one, but now I'm going to try something different to see if you like that, too!"

Today; One Day

Today

The rain has died

My shoes have died

The sun has died

My coat has died

The earth has died

Today.

One day

The rain will flower

My shoes will laugh

The sun will sing

My coat will fly

The earth will dance

One day.

from *Michael Rosen's Big Book of Bad Things*

I am very fond of this poem. It was inspired by a photo of a couple of people looking up at a tree. It's from World War II, and they are in a ghetto. When the Nazis came to power, they put Jewish people in the countries they occupied into parts of towns that were like huge open-air prisons. These people weren't allowed to leave, there were hardly any jobs, there was hardly any food, and bit by bit thousands of people died.

Looking at this photo with a group of children, I thought to myself that if I was going to write about it, I needed a kind of extreme writing that I call **impossible writing.**

The people in the photo are full of joy. And yet, because I know it was taken in a ghetto, it's a sad photo. I wanted to express all this in a short poem; I thought of the weather, the trees, and, because of some other well-known photos from this time, I thought of coats and shoes. I thought of despair and hope — hope and despair. Which way around should they go? A lot of stories from this time can be seen as full of despair. But we can't live on despair; we have to have hope, or there is no point in going on. So I decided to do despair first, and then hope.

"Today" is despair, because this couple knew people were dying around them — or, even worse, being taken off on railway trains never to be seen again. "Tomorrow" is hope. The people in the photo look happy and hopeful. There is fruit on the tree.

So with all these different elements in mind, I wrote the poem. As you can see, it's made up almost entirely of impossible writing: all those things in the poem can't *really* die, laugh, or sing. Tucked away in the back of my mind as I wrote were the paintings of Marc Chagall. He painted scenes from his childhood — a time when millions of Jews like him lived in the Russian and Polish countryside in small farms and villages. In his pictures happy people fly, and the colors suggest thriving, vibrant life. My own great-grandparents came from the places that Chagall painted, and other relatives of mine ended up in ghettos like the one in the photograph.

These are worlds that I was never part of — I was born safe and sound in London, after the Second World War was over. They're somehow on the other side, in a kind of dream-nightmare that's separate from me. At the same time, they're part of my family history. That's why it's "my" shoes and "my" coat that have "died."

But the world doesn't have to be like that. In fact, what happened to the Jewish people (and to millions of others) should never happen to anyone, anywhere. By saying "the earth will dance," I'm saying exactly that. It's not just me: it's not just my coat and shoes that will laugh and fly. The whole world will dance when there is no more genocide.

When I look back at a poem like this, I know that many people reading it won't get out of it what I've put into it. How could they? They might not have seen the photo I'm talking about, they won't know my family history, they might not know Chagall's pictures, and even if they do, they might not connect them to the poem or me.

So, do I think the poem is pointless? No. I think that if you write mysterious poems that have impossible writing in them, people will find meanings that are similar or related to your meanings. Maybe they will pick up on the contrast between despair and hope. Maybe they will see that there are ordinary things like coats and shoes alongside universal things like the sun and the earth, and they will see that the poem is about people and the world. Maybe all sorts of other pictures will come to their minds — street carnivals, music festivals, or famine followed by plenty.

That's all OK by me. Poems are a midway point between poets and readers. The poet pours in one set of meanings. The reader picks up the poem and puts in another set of meanings, and the two meet somewhere in the middle. That's what reading a poem is all about. It's a conversation between two sets of thoughts: the poet's and the reader's.

The Lift

At the second floor

we heard a voice inside the lift[1] say,

"Second floor, going up."

But the second floor

was the top floor.

Where were we going?

from *Michael Rosen's Big Book of Bad Things*

[1] **lift** elevator

I like finding poems or the start of poems in everyday life. As I go around, I find poems in all sorts of signs, notices, and directions, or I overhear people talking. One day, I was in an elevator and a voice said, "Second floor, going up." But I knew there was no floor higher than the second floor!

You could say it was just a mistake. The end. But then I started to imagine that there was a secret place higher up than the top floor, and that the elevator was going to go through the roof and just carry on — into the sky and then into space.

So, what started out as a kind of **found poem** turned into a little piece of science fiction. In the end, I didn't want to spell everything out. I wanted to leave the reader thinking *Where could the elevator go?*

And I like having a bit of a laugh at the way we are told that the language of official notices is correct and our conversations and chats are incorrect — messy and disorderly. So, when I come across official notices that are messy and disorderly, I like to collect them and have fun with them.

CHAPTER 4

WAYS TO START A POEM

One of the hardest things about writing poems can be getting started. Here are a few ideas. . . .

Daydream

One of the most important ways of starting to write is to daydream. Put yourself into a dreamy state and let your mind think about anything you like. You may find that it focuses on an object or an animal, or something that you've made up, something that you remember, something you wish for — or something else entirely. If at any point in your daydream you find a topic that could be fun to write about, make a note of it. You might be able to write about it straightaway, or you might want to save it for another time. I think daydreams are really, really great places to start a poem. It's just a matter of tuning into them.

Keep a Notebook

If you want to write poems, it's a good idea to keep a notebook and jot down anything you hear, see, or wonder about — a line from a song, an ad, something in a book you've read, something you heard on TV or on the bus. Write all of it down and then when you're thinking about poems, you can read back through and see if any of the things you wrote spark an idea. They often do.

Make Lists

What do you know best of all? Make a list of the things you know best: you could try the people in your family; the objects in your room; the places you go on vacation; your favorite sports, TV shows, foods, movies, books, songs, and so on.

Pick one of these things and focus on it as hard as you can. Start to daydream about it. Start thinking about what makes it special or different. What does it look, sound, smell, and feel like? How does it make you feel? Does it puzzle you? What does it make you wonder about? If it's a person, what sort of things does that person say?

Make a list of all the answers to those questions about the thing or person. Look at it. What happens if you remove the parts that don't sound interesting? What happens if you say a bit more to make some of the other parts more interesting? What happens if you change the order? What happens if you repeat some of the bits — does it give it a rhythm that you like? Have you got a good opening line you could repeat at the end? What happens if you put what you've written into short two-, three-, or four-word phrases like "chair falling" or "across the sky"?

I could write like that!

The easiest way to write a poem is to read a poem by someone else and then say to yourself, "I could write a poem like that."

When I say "like that," it could be that you imitate how it sounds, use the same rhythm or form, or write the same type of poem (such as a sonnet or a limerick).

Or it could be that you say to yourself, "This poem is about the poet's favorite food. I'll write a poem about *my* favorite food."

Or you could write about something that came to mind while you were reading the poem. You don't ever need to feel like you have to write in a particular way after you've read a poem. You can be inspired by any part of it: any sound that you like or any meaning that occurs to you.

You can do this with any poem you read in this book.

Pretend You're Someone Else

To pretend to be someone else, simply say, "I am . . ." and then put yourself into that person's shoes. You can choose someone you know, a famous person you've seen on TV or a character from another poem, story, movie, song, or wherever. Then, you can write a monologue for that person — as Robert Browning did in "My Last Duchess." You can imagine what they might say in a particular place at a particular time. You might want to think about what's bothering them, what they wish for, what makes them angry, what makes them jealous, what they're afraid of, what they might dream about. . . . It will help you to figure out what they were doing just before they were speaking your monologue — and what's going to happen next.

If you pretend you're an animal, you can ask yourself the same sort of questions. But the trick is that you are, in a way, thinking of the animal as if it were a person. That's pretty easy to do if you're pretending to be your pet. But you might want to try doing it with an animal you've seen in a zoo, or even an insect. In his poem "Clock-a-Clay," written more than two hundred years ago, John Clare (1793–1864) takes on the voice of a lady-bug. (In Northamptonshire, England, where he lived, "clock-a-clay" was a playful nickname for a ladybug.) Here's part of that poem:

In the cowslip pips I lie,
Hidden from the buzzing fly,
While green grass beneath me lies,
Pearled with dew like fishes' eyes,
Here I lie, a clock-a'-clay,
Waiting for the time o' day.

Or you could pretend to be an object: a sock, a TV, a railroad station — anything. Imagine you are that thing and ask yourself the same questions again: What can I see, what can I hear, and what are people saying? What am I thinking, and what do I dream about? What am I afraid of, what am I jealous of, what makes me angry, and what makes me happy?

Pick a Moment

A lot of poems are "in the moment." Pick a real moment you remember, or make one up.

Personal moments. Perhaps it's important to you because you did something great or something bad, or it made you unhappy . . . any kind of moment. You might start with a feeling—a moment when you were angry, sad, happy, jealous, envious, greedy, anxious, aggressive, nostalgic, euphoric, crazy, lost, bewildered, nervous, sorry, humiliated, ashamed . . . anything you really care about.

Now, the trick is to get yourself back into that moment. Try to live it again. You can write about it, using the words "I am," as if you are in the middle of it: "I am seeing . . . I am running . . ." Or you can write about it in the past, as a memory: "I was running . . . I sat down . . ." Or you can write about it as if you are someone else: "He is looking . . . She is dancing . . ."

To help you write, ask yourself: What could I see in that moment? What could I hear? What was I thinking, and what was I saying? What were other people saying? Why do I remember that moment so clearly? What makes it stick in my mind? Write down the answer to that question. Look at it. Does it make you want to add anything to what you've written or take anything away? Maybe it will, maybe it won't.

Moments in stories. You can find other kinds of moments in stories, movies, songs, dances, TV shows, or whatever. In every story we like, there is a moment or two that comes back to us as important, amazing, or mysterious. Freeze one of these and write what someone might be saying, singing, or thinking about it at the time. You can pretend you're inside that person's head and that you're writing down their stream of thoughts. You don't even have to write in sentences. Or you can have one person speaking a monologue and other people or things commenting on what's going on. For example, in the story of Hansel and Gretel, there's a moment when the children realize they've been abandoned in the forest. Think of the sights — the tall trees, the dark shadows. Think of the sounds — the rustling leaves, birdsong. You could decide to write a poem from the point of view of the birds: the audience will hear the words of the children through the ears of the birds, and then, every now and again, we'll hear the birds telling us what *they* think, or the trees talking as they bend toward the children, watching to see what will happen next.

Moments in conversations. Some of the most important moments in our lives happen when somebody says something to us, or we have a conversation with someone, or with a group of people.

We all remember an important conversation. But try to remember *why* you remember it! Why was it important? Write it down — maybe you'll want to put in some thoughts you had at the time. Maybe not. Try putting them in, then try taking them out. Maybe you'll want to say what you think about that conversation now. Maybe not. Try putting these thoughts in, then try taking them out.

Thinking about conversations can take you back to the most important moments of your life. Treasure them!

Start with a Picture

Some poems, like my poem "Today; One Day" (pages 106–107), begin with a painting or a photo. Pictures are good starting points for poems because they are freeze-frames that artists and photographers have made in order to say something interesting without using words.

You can pick a person, animal, or object in the picture and write down what he, she, or it is saying or thinking — or what they can see. Or you can try writing a conversation between people or objects in the picture; or write separate monologues, one for each person or object, and put them side by side.

Or you could try another approach. Let the picture "talk" to you and write down the stream of thoughts and feelings that come into your mind. You can then play with the words and phrases you used, repeating them and coming up with interesting rhythms. You might end up with something that is not about the picture or anything in the picture, but is inspired by the feelings you had when you looked at it.

Play with Dreams, Fantasies, and Nonsense

Poems are good ways to express our dreams, fantasies, and nonsense ideas.

Dreams You can try writing down your dreams in as direct and matter-of-fact a way as possible. Sometimes a stark, simple way of communicating something odd or fantastic is very effective. Or you might want to write from "within" the dream, telling it as it's happening, as if you're making a video diary: "Now I'm running along a high wall . . ."— that sort of thing. It may be if you do it this way, that you'll want to stop using whole sentences, and come up with something that sounds more breathless and broken up.

Fantasies Fantasies are our daydreams, things we would like to happen, or imagine could happen. Fantasy-fiction writers come up with amazing plots on a gigantic scale, where the forces of good and evil battle it out. Fantasy poems can be much smaller and more personal than that. They can be about wishes, desires, hopes, and transformations. One of the most famous of these is "Kubla Khan" by Samuel Taylor Coleridge (1772–1834). It's an extraordinary poem, full of powerful writing. Coleridge creates another land, and gives it a musical, dreamlike quality in the way he writes about it. Here's how the poem begins:

In Xanadu[1] did Kubla Khan[2]
A stately pleasure-dome decree:[3]
Where Alph, the sacred river, ran
Through caverns measureless to man
Down to a sunless sea.

[1] **Xanadu** a made-up place
[2] **Kubla Khan** the name of a king
[3] **decree** order to be built

You could try writing a modern "Kubla Khan." Or you could pick a real place you know (your school, town hall, or library?) and transform it into a fantastical land.

Nonsense You've been read nonsense poetry right from when you were very young, when you were told nursery rhymes. Think of "Hey Diddle Diddle": real worlds and impossible worlds intersect freely when a cow jumps over the moon, or when someone has a garden with silver bells and cockleshells in it. We looked at Edward Lear's nonsense poem "The Jumblies" earlier in the book (pages 56–61), and you may also have read nonsense poems by Lewis Carroll (1832–1898) or Shel Silverstein (1930–1999). A lot of them have very regular rhythms and rhymes, as if the poets are saying that the wildness of the nonsense looks and sounds best when it's organized into very regular, straight-sounding verses. Lewis Carroll's "Jabberwocky" is an example of this. Here's the beginning:

'Twas brillig, and the slithy toves
Did gyre and gimble in the wabe:
All mimsy were the borogoves,
And the mome raths outgrabe.

You don't have to follow that pattern, but it's worth a try. See if you can come up with an odd or strange story, with a mix of made-up creatures and real ones. Or you could try making objects come alive — maybe your fridge, or a cake. Then think of a plot or a short story that these characters are involved in. A fight? A love affair? Has something been stolen? Are they on a journey? Do they get lost? Now see if you can give the story a regular rhythm and rhyme, perhaps using a chorus, too. The chorus might be made up of nonsense words that you've invented but that seem to have something to do with the main story that you're telling.

Celebrate Your Culture and Traditions

Poems can be places to write about how we live and whom we belong to. This is sometimes called our culture or our tradition. We can ask questions about our culture, and sometimes the answers give us poems. Write your answers one under the other. Are they interesting as a list, or do you need to add something or change the words to give it a rhythm? Here are some things you could think about:

Home What makes your home special? What do you like about it? What don't you like about it? What do people say about it? What would you do to improve it? Think of a few things you can see in your home as you sit and daydream about it. Do you have a bad memory or a good memory of one of these things? How can you write about that memory in a way that's interesting? You could write as if you were one of those things: a wall, or a stovetop, or a floor. Maybe this thing has memories from before you lived in your home. Try imagining them and writing them down.

Food What's your favorite food? Who makes it? Where does it come from? What does it smell and taste like? Can you remember special occasions when you ate that food, what people said at the time, and what you were thinking?

Sayings These are the special things your family and friends say: proverbs; catchphrases; riddles; jokes; memories; stuff they say over and over again; things they say when they are angry, hungry, happy, worried, going out, coming home, and so on. You might find a list of them is a poem! Here are a few things people have said that I've collected to put in poems:

My hair's a mess.
You look awful.
No, you can't come with me!
Come *on*.
HEEELP!
He started it.

Games What about games you play? Can you capture in words what it's like to play a particular game? Imagine yourself in the moment of playing. What are you thinking? What are you saying? What are other people saying? What feels special about the game and the things you use in it?

Festivals What about festivals and special days, such as birthdays? Think of the things you and your family celebrate and your memories of past celebrations. What did you eat? Can you remember when something important, odd, or funny happened? Take us to that moment. What were people doing? What were they saying? What were you thinking? What could you see going on around you?

Look at your answers to all these different questions. Are they interesting as a list or do you need to add something or change the words to give it a rhythm?

Do you need to add any details to help someone reading see these things for themselves? Can you write about a memory in a way that makes the reader feel like they're actually there? If you shuffle lines around or repeat them, do they start to make a shape or rhythm that you like?

Chapter 5

Writing Poems

Once you have an idea for a poem — a daydream, a moment, an object you like, an event or a happening — you might want to try out different ways of writing it down.

Talk with Your Pen

Try writing as if you're talking. You could begin with "Hey, I was thinking about . . ." then let it flow — "talk" it onto the page. Look at what you've written. Have you said everything you want to say? Is there anything you'd like to add? Or perhaps you've said too much! That's possible, too. Maybe you want it to be a bit mysterious, or to leave your readers wondering. Maybe you need to tell us a few more details so that we get a good picture of where the poem's set, or what the person speaking is thinking.

Less Is More

Quite often, what we like about poems is that they're short and to the point; they say big things in as quick a way as possible. Sometimes a few words can express more feeling or more wisdom than a great many. You can say a lot with **impression writing** — that is, writing in what I call non-sentences. If I'm writing about my cat, I might make a list of phrases that describe what he does, what he looks like, and what he sees — and that might make a poem.

Scratch on the door
Whiskers twitching
Tail flicks
Up in the sky, a bird

Impossible Writing

A man is asleep on a park bench. Let's say you want to write a poem about this that surprises readers and captures their interest. You can reverse the idea that the man is lying on the bench and suggest that, somehow or another, the bench is holding or supporting the man.

The park bench is carrying a sleeping man
The sky drags the trees up high

Of course, the bench isn't really carrying the man, nor is the sky dragging the trees up — but to say that they are surprises us. It can be fun to experiment with impossible writing about things you see and hear. And if you're thinking of writing about something very sad or tragic, impossible writing can make it seem as though everything's so awful that even your words have ended up sounding impossible.

The Chorus

One of the easiest ways to start a poem is by thinking up a chorus. Imagine, say, that you're at the swimming pool. Then think of a chorus — "water up my nose" or "splash splosh," for example. Now think about what's happening at the pool. What can you see? What can you hear? What are you saying? What are other people saying? What are you thinking? What are you feeling?

Write down the answers to these questions in a list, and in between every two or three lines, you can put your chorus. How does it sound? If it feels as if you're saying the chorus too often, cut out a few of them. If it feels like you don't need it, you can cut it out altogether. Or you might want more of the chorus as it gives your poem a shape or a good rhythm.

Thinking of a chorus first works well for writing about a public place such as a swimming pool, a movie theater, or an airport, but it also works well for private places, like your room; for moments in time, like breakfast time; for a car trip, or a very tiny event like catching a fly or running in a race. It seems to give the poem a scaffold, which you can decide to keep, change, or get rid of, depending on how you feel. The other good thing about choruses is that when you perform a poem with a chorus, people in the audience can join in. Here's one of my own chorus poems:

After Dark

Outside after dark,

trains hum and traffic lights wink,

after dark, after dark.

In here after dark,

curtains shake and closets creak,

after dark, after dark.

Under the covers after dark,

I twiddle my toes and hug my pillow,

after dark, after dark.

from *Bananas in My Ears*

Call and Response

Call and response is when one person says something, and then everyone replies with a chorus line. When sailors had to work together to pull ropes, it helped them if they sang what are known as **sea shanties,** which use call and response. People in Christian churches have used this form too, as have men in chain gangs (lines of prisoners chained together and forced to carry out hard labor like breaking stones or digging fields). A sea shanty might have the response line "haul 'em away," which everyone shouts, chants, or sings. The caller can say what they see, think, dream about, are afraid of, or whatever.

You could think up a call and response for, let's say, taking an exam. Your **response** line could be something ordinary like "Sitting in the exam hall," or something more fun like "We don't know the answer." Your **calls** could be things like "I've studied till my eyes are red," "My pen's running out," or "I can't remember anything."

Question and Answer

You can write poems that are a series of questions and answers — some examples of this are the old riddle poems, such as "I Gave My Love a Cherry," and the one below, about a boy who tricked the Devil on the road.

> ***Devil*: "What is that on your back?"**
> ***Boy*: "My bundles and my books."**
> ***Devil*: "Whose are these sheep and cattle?"**
> ***Boy*: "They are mine and my mother's."**
> ***Devil*: "How many of them are mine?"**
> ***Boy*: "Those that have blue tails."**

A more modern example is "Who Killed Davey Moore?," a song by Bob Dylan, which asks who was responsible for the death of a boxer after a fight. It's written in the style of an old nursery rhyme that asks who killed a robin.

"Who killed Cock Robin?"
"I," said the Sparrow,
"With my bow and arrow,
I killed Cock Robin."

To make these poems work, you have to decide who's asking the questions and who's giving the answers. You might find that either the question or the answer is the same — or nearly the same — each time.

Question-and-answer poems can be about tragic or awful things, or they can be about funny, absurd, loving things or philosophical problems. The great thing about them is that they don't have to give a final, all-answering answer! They can leave the reader or listener with plenty to think about.

Wordplay

Here's a counting-out rhyme for young children:

Eena meena

macka racka

rare rah

dominacka

chicka bocka

lolly poppa

OM

POM

PUSH!

It's good fun to say this in different ways — fast, slow, loud, quiet. It reminds me that one enjoyable thing to do with words is play with them. You can start with real words and make up words that sound like them. Or you can start with words that don't exist and make them sound like they might. Let's begin with the word *pepper.* You can break a part of the word out and say:

Pep, pep, pepper.

And you can add bits to that:

Peppy, peppy, pepper.

Then you can change some of the vowels:

Pip, pap, peep, pepper.

And you can slip in one or two other consonants:

Pipply, papply, popply, pepper.

Now, to have a bit more fun, you could put this nonsense into sensible surroundings. How about a restaurant, and someone asking for salt and pepper with their meal?

"Excuse me, waiter, could I have some salt
and pepper with my vegetables?"
"Yes, sir, would that be:
the pep, pep, pepper
or the peppy, peppy, pepper,
or the pip, pap, peep, pepper,
or the pipply, papply, popply, pepper?"
"I'll just have the salt, thanks."

On the next page you'll find a wordplay poem I wrote.

The Button Bop

Top button
Bottom button
Top button
Top.

Bottom button
Top button
Bottom button
Bop.

Top, top
Bottom button top
Bop, bop
Bottom button bop.

from *A Great Big Cuddle*

Imagism

As you write, try making a strict rule for yourself—you can say anything to do with what you see, but nothing about what you hear, smell, touch, or taste. And, more importantly, you can't write down what you think or feel. Somehow, by writing down what you see, you must express a feeling without saying what that feeling is. So, let's say you're describing a very dull, rainy day in a park in autumn. It's near the end of the day, and people are going home, the leaves are falling off the trees, water is slipping down the drains, and clouds are closing in. . . . If you put all that together, can you convey something a bit sad without saying "I'm sad"?

In my poem "Over My Toes," I wanted to create a calm, dreamy, happy feeling without telling people what to feel outright:

Over My Toes

Over my toes

goes

the soft sea wash

see the sea wash

the soft sand slip

see the sea slip

the soft sand slide

see the sea slide

the soft sand slap

see the sea slap

the soft sand wash

over my toes.

from *Bananas in My Ears*

This kind of writing is known as **imagism.** You can play it like a game: when you've written one of these poems, get someone else to guess the emotion you were trying to convey.

Symbolism

Any animal, object, or activity can be written about in a way that makes it represent or **symbolize** something else. One of the first poems I ever wrote was about a square meter of ground on the side of a hill in France in summer. The more I wrote about the spiky grass and plants, the thorns, and the ants running around, the more it seemed like a battlefield. And in a way, there was a battle going on between the sun trying to dry out the plants, and the plants resisting and keeping the water in their roots and leaves. And, as I said, it was all spiky. So this little meter of ground came to represent a battle — it became symbolic of it.

A million scrapes and sharpenings
form each scale of every plated body

that swarms through the daggered scrub.

Michael Rosen, sixteen years old

Now, I didn't start out thinking that this was how I was going to write. I only discovered that I wanted it to be a battle about halfway through trying to describe the plants and the ants. But in the back of my mind, I must have had a vague idea that the thing I was describing could represent something else.

Try thinking and writing about, say, a family car trip, bubbles in a bottle of seltzer water, or the marks on a stone. See if by thinking about what one of these things looks, sounds, smells, and feels like, you start to get an idea of what it might represent.

Long and Short

Here's a writing experiment that I tried once, and I don't know why it worked! I divided a group of people up into "longs" and "shorts." I came up with a subject: the street. The shorts could only describe something going on in the street with one word or two. The longs were allowed to use five, six, or seven words. Then the longs and shorts took turns reading aloud what they had made up. We experimented with having two shorts, then a long. And then we tried two shorts and two longs. Then three shorts and one long. It turned out that two shorts and one long worked best. After that, everyone sat down and made up new descriptions, or put the ones that they'd said into some sort of order. They found that if they repeated some of the short lines, it gave the whole thing a rhythm.

As I said, I have no idea why it worked. But it really did. Everyone found it very easy to do, and we had a street-picture poem very quickly — and with a great deal of fun. And the rhythm and excitement of the street was somehow in the poem, too.

Red bricks, bright lights,
Windows reflecting the sun.
Bright lights, lights change,
Clouds peeping over the tops of flats.[1]

[1] **flats** apartments

Lights change, red bricks,

A man starts to walk into the shop, stops . . .

then walks away.

Red bricks, bright lights.

Volcano Page

I was once listening to the radio, and a woman from the island of Montserrat, in the Caribbean, was talking about living on the side of a volcano. The interviewer asked her if she was afraid: after all, most of her fellow islanders had left and refused to come back. "No," she said, "because I have my volcano bag." "What's that?" asked the interviewer. And the woman said that it was a bag hanging from a hook by her front door. In the bag were all the things she would need if she had to run away from the volcano quickly.

I've often thought about that, and it gave me an idea for writing a poem. Imagine you have a volcano bag because a nearby volcano could blow at any minute. But instead of a bag, you've got a volcano page. Then write down what you want to put on your volcano page in case of disaster. Now, of course, you can put down things like a bottle of water, medicine, and that sort of practical thing—but write down some other things you need for survival, such as: your best memory, a favorite line from a favorite song, a hope for what you might become in life, a hope for what might become of your family, a fear of what might happen to you or your family, a scene from a book or film, something someone said to you that you thought was wise or useful or hopeful.

Do all the things you've written down make sense as a list? Or do you need to add some things so that they make sense? And could your poem do with being given a rhythm or shape in some way? Perhaps you could try repeating parts of it. Or you could give it a kind of chorus like "this I need" or "I live with this." Or perhaps the rhythm could come from repeating something like "he said," "she said," or "the song said."

This could then end up as a poem about your **philosophy** (your personal world outlook), but you haven't said that's what it is. It's just come about by collecting fragments and lines you've heard and read, and putting them together with your memories.

Things To Do with Your Poems

What you *do* with a poem you write is as important as writing it—we learn from how others react to our poems. The question is, who is going to read and hear your poems, and how are they going to get ahold of them?

The simplest and easiest thing to do is to find someone you know and respect and **read them your poem,** or leave it with them to read in their own time. You may or may not like what they say afterward. If it's a close friend or member of your family, you have to factor in that they may be being nice about it because they're fond of you and don't want to hurt your feelings; or that they might be tough on you because they don't want to coddle you.

You can publish your poetry yourself, either by starting a **poetry blog** and posting your poems there, or by printing them out and making some kind of booklet to give away or sell. You can get together with one or more people and create a group poetry blog, or make a booklet or magazine together and give it away or sell it.

You can think about **performing** your poems. To start off with, you could try reading them at a family event — or you could try to organize a **poetry event** at your school that mixes poetry with dance or music, maybe with some art or photography projected onto a screen.

It's easy to create a **poetry wall.** Simply write out your poems in an attractive and interesting way and put them up on a wall. You can do this on your own or with other people. It looks great when you put poems with drawings.

There are **poetry clubs** in most big cities and towns. It's worth going along first to see and hear what other poets are doing, and then think about reading a poem when they have an opening for new poets. These clubs are good places to take the poems you've published in magazines or booklets. If you or your parents think you are too young for this, ask if the club could have a children's poetry evening.

You can **make videos** of yourself or someone else reading your poems and post them online, or show them at school or at events such as celebrations.

Look out for **book and literature festivals** nearby. They might be interested in an evening when local people read their poems, or an evening of children and young people's poems. See if you can get in touch with the organizers to suggest this.

Youth groups — such as drama, dance, and youth clubs — might be interested in doing something with your poems. You could suggest having an evening or a show where poetry is mixed in with drama, dance, or social events.

Look for one-off poetry events in theaters, arts centers, and concert halls nearby. If you've started a poetry blog, you could review poetry events and perhaps get to know the organizers — then see if they would be prepared to put on an event that involves children and young people. Look out for **poetry slams** near you. These are fantastic fun, and they might have a young people's slam you could take part in.

When you're thinking of a poetry event, there are some key things to remember:

- Not too many poems! I would say that on any poetry evening, you shouldn't have more than two twenty-minute sets. That is, two sessions, each one twenty minutes long, when people read poems.

- Make sure everyone can see well and hear clearly. You need to have a good microphone and speaker set up, and make sure the room is well lit or that there are stage lights.

- Think about what else you can have in addition to poems: forty minutes is a bit short for a whole evening. Music is good! So what kind of music? Jazz works well, and so do solos, duets, and trios of classical music. And singing — choir, or solo, or both. You could have a dance performance as well.

- Think of visuals: you could have a screen where you show drawings, paintings, photos, or videos.

- You could add in some sketches, which are short comedy pieces performed by a small group of actors. You could try parodies of things on TV, newly written songs, or little scenes.

- Some children and young people attend dance and music classes where they learn material from cultures other than the ones they come across in school. It's really great to make this part of an evening, too.

- It's hard to organize or think about events on your own. Get your parents, older brothers and sisters, teachers, adult organizers of clubs, and people at arts centers to help you. If you show them my suggestions and discuss your ideas with them, you'll find they have plenty of suggestions of their own. The most important thing is to get up and running and put on at least one event.

- You could think about setting up a poetry group that simply reads poems to one another. Don't do it too often, or you won't keep it up. Once a month at the very most!

I promise you that the effect of any or all of this is that it will get you thinking long and hard about what you want to write and how to write it. You will think about whether you really want to perform your poems, or whether you would like someone else to perform them. If you can get even a small group — two, three, or four of you — sharing poems, it will help you enormously.

Chapter 6

Some Technical Points about Poems

This is far from being a full list. That would take a thousand-page dictionary! I've just selected a few topics you may come across at school, along with some others that you might find useful to think about.

Rhythm and Rhyme

Poems are made up of strings of words. For any piece of writing or speaking to make sense, you need a sequence of words — not just single words floating about aimlessly in midair.

And the moment you string words together, you not only start to make sense — you start to make rhythms. You create echoes between words that sound a bit like each other — and patterns you can play with in all sorts of ways. So, if I say, "The cat sat on the mat," you can hear that three of these words sound alike. If I say, "The cat sat on the mat, the cat sat on the mat, the cat sat on the mat," you can hear that the words fit a rhythm. If I say, "The cat sat on the dog," then you might be surprised, because you were expecting the usual sequence that ends in "mat." If I say, "The cat sat on the mat, the plate sat on the shelf," you can hear that the sequence has the same rhythm, but the words have changed. The new words have slotted into the pattern provided by "the cat sat on the mat." It's as if each part of the sequence is a place for new words to go into, a bit like spaces on a chessboard.

Poets have invented many rhythms over the years. Some are as regular as clockwork, with beats and off-beats that fit exactly into a time. Regular poems have sections that go, for example, "tee-**TUM**" again and again. If I write:

> **Today, today, today, today, today,**
> **You cried, you cried, you cried, you cried,**
> **you cried.**

You can see it goes "tee-**TUM,** tee-**TUM,** tee-**TUM,** tee-**TUM,** tee-**TUM**" and then repeats that. There are five tee-**TUMs** in each line.

Believe it or not, there's a word to describe that kind of rhythm. Each tee-**TUM** is called an **iamb,** and a five-beat line is called **pentameter**. So **iambic pentameter** describes my piece of writing about "today."

The only problem is that I don't think it's very good! In other words, I can write in "perfect" iambic pentameter, but it doesn't make a very interesting line of poetry. The challenge (if I want it) is to write really good poetry in iambic pentameter.

An iamb is an example of what is called a **foot** in poetry, as if poems were made up of footsteps. There are many kinds of rhythmic feet: *Humpty Dumpty,* for example, goes "**TUM**-tee, **TUM**-tee." *Catapult* goes "**TUM-TUM**-tee." *Football* goes "**TUM-TUM.**" And *happily* goes "**TUM**-tee-tee." The **TUM** bit is called a **stress,** which marks out where a beat comes in a line.

Each of these different kinds of feet has a name. But I can't promise you that knowing what they are or what they are called will help you write good poems. They are quite handy if a musician asks you to write some lyrics, but most people can just feel a rhythm without knowing anything technical about it.

Some poems have a regular rhythm and no rhyme. This is called **blank verse.** Some poems have neither a regular rhythm nor a regular rhyme. This is called **free verse.** It's been said that the foot of a free-verse poem is one whole line. So if you're writing free verse, you can think of each line as a single unit that hangs together because it creates a meaning.

There are many different ways to make poems rhyme. The rhyming words can come at the end of a line of the same number of beats and offbeats:

tee-**TUM,** tee-**TUM,** tee-**TUM,** tee-**BOAT.** A
tee-**TUM,** tee-**TUM,** tee-**TUM,** tee-**FLOAT.** A
tee-**TUM,** tee-**TUM,** tee-**TUM,** tee-**PLACE.** B
tee-**TUM,** tee-**TUM,** tee-**TUM,** tee-**FACE.** B

These lines have a pattern of rhymes, which is called its **rhyme scheme.** Here, the first two lines rhyme: you can label them both "A." Then, the next two lines rhyme—but it's a new rhyme, so you can call them "B." So the rhyme scheme of this piece of writing is **AABB.**

Now look at this:

There was a Young Lady whose chin, A
Resembled the point of a pin; A
So she had it made sharp, B
And purchased a harp, B
And played several tunes with her chin. A

Edward Lear

This poem is a **limerick:** its rhyme scheme is **AABBA.** In limericks, the rhythm changes partway through. You have two three-feet lines, followed by two two-feet lines, finishing with one three-feet line.

There are various ways to rhyme words. You can rhyme single whole words like *boat* and *float*. You can rhyme two syllables, like *drummer* and *summer.* Or you can make a **half rhyme** that rhymes part of one word with part of another, like in *dinner* and *summer* (just the *-er* sound rhymes), or *party* and *carter* (*par-* and *car-*), or even *farm* and *worm,* or *night* and *bought*. Pop songs and raps don't bother about being too exact, and they end up rhyming things like *cried* and *night.*

There's also something called **internal rhyme,** which is when a rhyming word comes in the middle of a line, rather than at the end. In the poem below, *woke* makes the internal rhyme.

Just as a joke,

I woke up a bloke[1],

[1] **bloke** man

who was driving me mad at night.
He snored,
then he roared
and we both ended up in a fight.

Sound Techniques

As well as rhythm and rhyme, poets play with sounds, often repeating them in ways that help poems to stick in people's minds. You can repeat a consonant at the beginning of a word or the first stressed syllable of a word. If I say, "Big Bill Broonzy was a blues singer," you can hear that the *b* sound is repeated at the beginning of the three parts of his name.

Here are the opening lines of "The Deep-Sea Cables" by Rudyard Kipling (1865–1936):

The wrecks dissolve above us;
their dust drops down from afar —
Down to the dark, to the utter dark,
where the blind white sea-snakes are.

See how the letter *d* is repeated at the beginning of words? This is called **alliteration.**

Sound can also work to link words and meanings, or to give an impression of whatever it is the poem is describing. When W. H. Auden wrote about the "pluck" and "knock of the tide," I think he wanted to make it so that the *ck* sound of "pluck" and "knock" sounds like a wave when it slaps the beach.

Assonance is when a vowel sound is repeated. The poet Gerard Manley Hopkins talked of "weeds in wheels." The *ee* sound is repeated, which links the words "weeds" and "wheels" together: it makes me think of weeds growing up between the spokes of an old wheel left lying in a field. Assonance can help the rhythm of a line — and of a whole poem.

Metaphor and Simile

When we're writing, we put different images together all the time — people, animals, or things. We describe one thing in terms of another: being the other thing, or being like the other thing. This is called using **metaphor,** and it can be done in common, ordinary ways ("He's an angel" or "You're a star," for example), but it can also be done in extraordinary and unexpected ways.

When a metaphor uses *like* or *as* to directly compare two images, it's called a **simile.** William Wordsworth begins his poem "Daffodils" with the line "I wandered lonely as a cloud." The idea of a person wandering and being lonely is quite common, but bringing the cloud into it creates something unusual. Are clouds lonely? What kinds of cloud are lonely? And is the "I" in the poem lonely in the same way? The comparison gets us thinking.

Shakespeare's play *Richard III* famously begins with Richard saying:

Now is the winter of our discontent.
Made glorious summer by this son of York.

Discontent doesn't really have seasons. Shakespeare's using winter as a metaphor, giving an idea of coldness and the worst moment of "discontent." But the good news is that the winter's been turned to summer (metaphorically). Richard's been cheered up by the "son of York" becoming king — by which Shakespeare means the eldest son (Richard's brother Edward) of an aristocratic family, the House of York. He's playing with words here: *son* sounds like *sun,* summer has sun, and King Edward's symbol is a sun.

Metonymy

The person who runs a meeting is often called the chair. The word *chair* stands for the person sitting in the chair. This is called **metonymy.** Metonymy is when one thing is used to stand for something else that it's related to. But when I use the word *chair* to mean a person, do I, in some deeper way, make that person seem immobile — a bit like a chair? Perhaps. Perhaps not.

If you wanted to write about being lost in the supermarket when you were very little (let's say three or four years old), you might write about people as "feet" or "legs" to convey that all you could see were their feet and legs.

Personification

You'll remember that in Tennyson's poem "The Eagle" (page 21), he writes about the eagle as if it were an ancient king. **Personification** suggests that things, animals, feelings, ideas, and thoughts can behave in ways people behave. As we saw on pages 78–79, Thomas Hardy writes about snowflakes losing their way. Snowflakes can't really get lost, but it makes sense when he likens them to people.

Personification is also a way of giving the world around us feelings that we ourselves have, wish to have, or are afraid that we have. In a blizzard, snowflakes are blown about in all directions, some upward instead of downward as if they're going the wrong way — and this

reminds me of a time when I was lost. So because of personification, a poem that seems to be about something outside of us can contain hidden messages about our inner selves.

Persona

Beware when a poet says "I": the "I" is not the poet. When a poet writes a poem, he or she often puts on a special poem-telling voice, and the "I" is built up of the words the poet has chosen. But a poet is a person, not words. We call the character telling the poem the poet's **persona.** There's an example of this in the poem on the next two pages, "Where Go the Boats?" by Robert Louis Stevenson.

Where Go the Boats?

Dark brown is the river.

    Golden is the sand.

It flows along for ever,

    With trees on either hand.

Green leaves a-floating,

    Castles of the foam,

Boats of mine a-boating –

    Where will all come home?

On goes the river

And out past the mill,

Away down the valley,

Away down the hill.

Away down the river,

A hundred miles or more,

Other little children

Shall bring my boats ashore.

Robert Louis Stevenson

The person speaking in the poem is a child playing with boats. We can put together a description of that child — but to be true to how poetry works, we should use only evidence that we find in the poem. In "Where Go the Boats?," the child seems to enjoy the landscape around the river where he or she is playing — we can't be absolutely sure if it's a "he" or a "she." This child has one big question: "Where will the boats end up?" And the persona leaves us wondering with him or her about the possibility of "other little children" far away finding the boats.

Sometimes there is no "I" or "my" to guide us to the persona behind a poem. Take a look at Thomas Hardy's poem "At the Railway Station, Upway."

At the Railway Station, Upway

"There is not much that I can do,
For I've no money that's quite my own!"
Spoke up the pitying child—
A little boy with a violin
At the station before the train came in,—
"But I can play my fiddle to you,
And a nice one 'tis, and good in tone!"

The man in the handcuffs smiled;
The constable looked, and he smiled, too,
As the fiddle began to twang;
And the man in the handcuffs suddenly sang
Uproariously:
"This life so free
Is the thing for me!"
And the constable smiled, and said no word,
As if unconscious of what he heard;
And so they went on till the train came in—
The convict, and boy with the violin.

Thomas Hardy

We're given one or two hints about the persona when Hardy writes, "till the train came in." "Came in" suggests that he wants us to think of the person speaking as a silent witness at a station, watching events. In other words, the persona of the poem is like a journalist or even a photographer — a watcher who isn't affecting what they see. This gives the poem a strange, unemotional quality. And yet what is going on is a very emotional encounter between a prisoner, a boy with a violin, and a policeman on a station platform.

Allusion

Some poems are in a kind of conversation with other poems or other stories: we call this **allusion.** In *Alice's Adventures in Wonderland,* by Lewis Carroll, there are several poems that Alice hears strange people and creatures reciting. Most of them are really poking fun at other poems. Here's one of them:

How Doth the Little Crocodile

How doth the little crocodile

Improve his shining tail,

And pour the waters of the Nile

On every golden scale!

How cheerfully he seems to grin

How neatly spreads his claws

And welcomes little fishes in

With gently smiling jaws!

Lewis Carroll

At first, the poem seems to be celebrating the crocodile for being so good at pouring water on his tail! But children who went to Sunday school at the time when the Alice books came out would have been very familiar with a poem published in 1715 that begins like this:

How doth the little busy bee
Improve each shining hour,
And gather honey all the day
From every opening flower!

from "Against Idleness and Mischief"
by **Isaac Watts** (1674–1748)

This is what might be called a "good example." In Sunday school, children were always told that "idle hands make mischief" and that it was right and good to be busy. The bee was a good example of how to be busy. If you are busy, the poem says, you will get rich. But Lewis Carroll's poem seems to be making fun of the idea by suggesting something quite different. A predatory, dangerous animal goes about making himself look golden and shiny so that he can seduce and gobble up fish.

These two poems are obviously related, but in a way *all* poems have links with other pieces of writing, using forms, metaphors, similes, plot lines, and personas that have appeared elsewhere. So if I write a limerick, it's linked to all the other limericks that have been written because it's in the same shape as them.

Poems

Chapter 7

So What Is Poetry?

I have decided to leave the next five pages blank for you to write any answers you'd like. If the answers you come up with work for you, then they're the right answers. Maybe something I've said in the previous chapters will help!

Appendix

Just as important as reading anything I've written in this book is for you to read poems and go see poets performing. Do this as often as you can, and as often as is enjoyable.

If you have an arts center anywhere near you, find out if any poets who you might be interested in are reading their poems there. Ask in your local library: they may have a poetry circle and might like to set up an evening that would be suitable for children and young people.

The library is also the place to start when it comes to poetry books. Talk to a librarian about books that might be suitable for you to read. Spend time just browsing and looking. No one ever finds the poems they like straightaway.

There are thousands of poems online. Most poems by famous authors who died before 1930 are online. All you have to do is put their name into a search engine.

There are some special sites to do with poetry. Here are some of the best:

The Children's Poetry Archive:
www.childrenspoetryarchive.org

Poetryline: www.clpe.org.uk/poetryline

Young Poets Network:
ypn.poetrysociety.org.uk

The Poetry Archive: www.poetryarchive.org

Poetry by Heart: www.poetrybyheart.org.uk

Poetry Foundation: www.poetryfoundation.org

Poetry Daily: poems.com

The Poetry Society: poetrysociety.org.uk

SLAMbassadors UK:
slam.poetrysociety.org.uk

Academy of American Poets: www.poets.org

TweetSpeak Poetry: www.tweetspeakpoetry.com

The Poetry Zone: poetryzone.co.uk

The Writer's Almanac: writersalmanac.org

Poetry Translation Centre:
www.poetrytranslation.org

Discovering Poetry:
www.discoveringpoetry.co.uk
Poetry 180: www.loc.gov/poetry/180
Poetry Live!: poetrylive.net
Tower Poetry: www.towerpoetry.org.uk
Archive of the Now:
www.archiveofthenow.org

There are also lots of videos of poets performing their poems online. Here's where to find them:

Poems Out Loud: poemsoutloud.net/video
The Poetry Station: www.poetrystation.org.uk
London Poetry Systems on Vimeo:
www.vimeo.com/channels/lps
Video section of Apples and Snakes:
www.applesandsnakes.org/page/43/Poetry+Films
Video section of Poetry Foundation:
www.poetryfoundation.org/features/video

If you're interested in buying poetry books — in addition to borrowing them from the library — try an independent bookshop first, as these usually have the biggest range of poetry books.

If you find that you like a poem you've read in this book or in a book at school, see if there are any collections of poems by the person who wrote it. You may well find that you like more of their poems.

The best book I know that covers the technical side of poetry is the *Princeton Encyclopedia of Poetry and Poetics*. Stephen Fry's book *The Ode Less Travelled: Unlocking the Poet Within* discusses how you can write poems by starting out from this technical side.

Check out what poetry books your school has. You can ask the librarian *and* the English teachers what poetry books they have.

Index

Acknowledgments

"Today; One Day" and "The Lift" © 2010 by Michael Rosen, taken from *Michael Rosen's Big Book of Bad Things* by Michael Rosen (London: Puffin, 2010). Reproduced by permission of Penguin Books Ltd.

"Snow in the Suburbs" from *Complete Poems of Thomas Hardy* by Thomas Hardy. Copyright © 1978 by Macmillan London, Ltd. Reprinted with the permission of Scribner, a division of Simon & Schuster, Inc. All rights reserved.

"I Am Angry" and "The Button Bop" © 2015 by Michael Rosen, taken from *A Great Big Cuddle* by Michael Rosen. Reproduced by permission of Candlewick Press.

"Feeling Ill," "Fooling Around," "After Dark," and "Over My Toes" © 1986, 1987 by Michael Rosen. Taken from *Bananas in My Ears* by Michael Rosen. Reproduced by permission of Candlewick Press.